NATIONAL GEOGRAPHIC
Little Kids™
WORD BOOK

LEARNING THE WORDS IN YOUR WORLD

seashell

apple

Jim Bear

tiger

steamroller

NATIONAL GEOGRAPHIC

WASHINGTON, D.C.

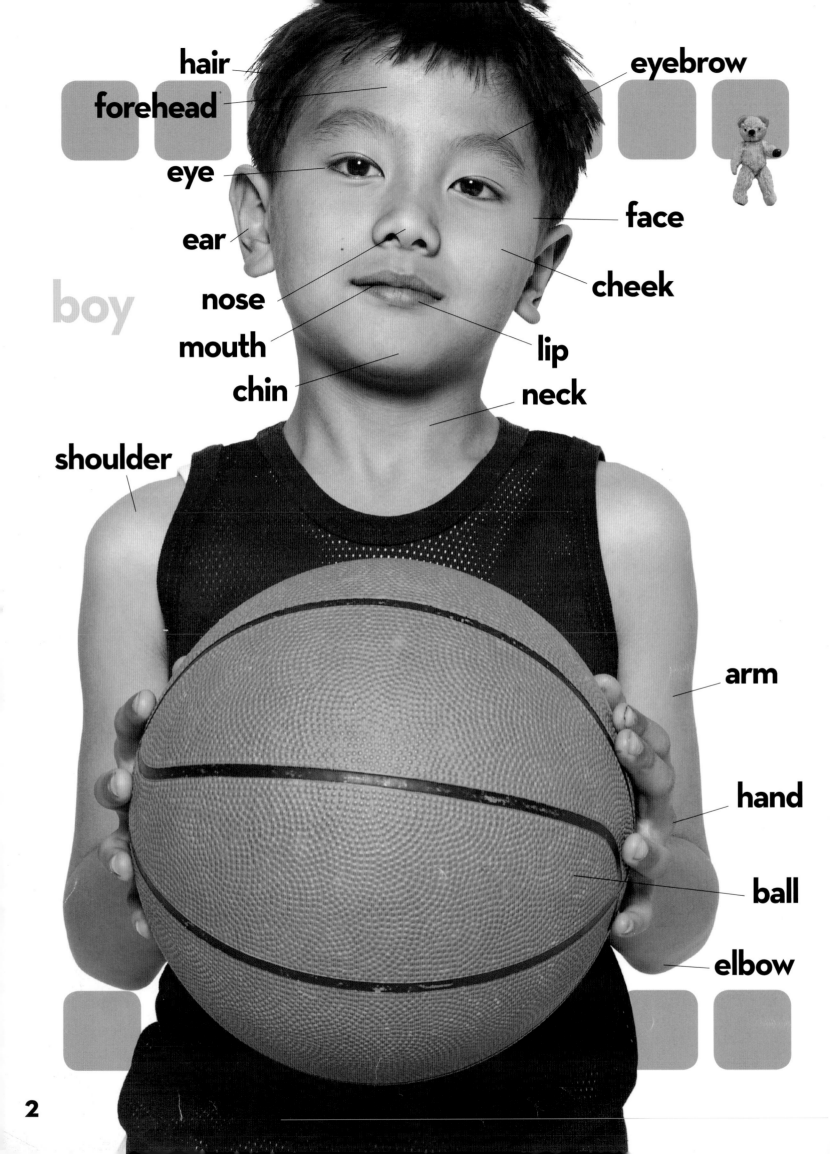

boy

hair

eyebrow

forehead

eye

face

ear

cheek

nose

mouth

lip

chin

neck

shoulder

arm

hand

ball

elbow

2

CONTENTS

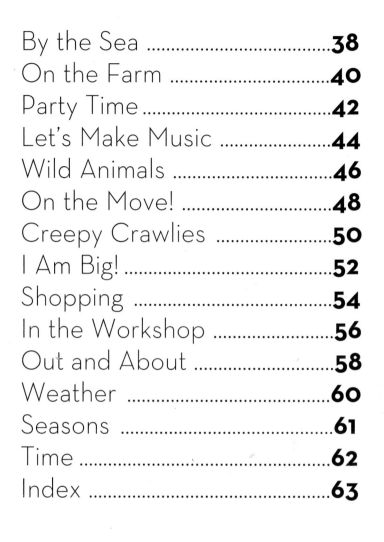

Betty Bear

HOW TO USE THIS BOOK

What pattern is the girl's **dress**?

What color is the **polar bear**?

face

hair

arm

finger

elbow

thumb

girl

dress

hand

knee

leg

ankle

shoes

Word Book has been created especially for young children. It will give them a head start in learning vital preschool skills such as language and number recognition. It includes the words that children are most familiar with by the age of five. Bright, colorful photographs of familiar and unusual objects, animals, and places will help to widen their knowledge of the world around them. Each section has its own theme, to help young children make the connections between words and pictures.

polar bear

Counting
You can practice your numbers by counting the objects along the bottom of each page!

Young children like to look at pictures and love naming what they see. It is even more fun for them to share a word book with an adult. Start by talking about what is in the picture, and what the object might be used for. Talk about colors and shapes. Look at the scale of the objects—they might be very different on different pages. You can use the questions around the edges of the pages to start a conversation and encourage the child to study the pictures more closely. When they are familiar with the book, show them the index in the back, and explain how it is organized alphabetically.

A Note for Kids

Jim and Betty Bear are hidden on each page of this book. Look closely and see if you can spot them. How many did you count?

(see answer on page 64)

Jim Bear

Betty Bear

hair

eyebrow

eye

nose

boy

shirt

ALPHABET LETTERS

What words can you spell using the alphabet?

A a

B b

C c

D d

E e

F f

G g

H h

I i

J j

K k

L l

M m

A A A A A A

How many letters are in the alphabet?

N n

O o

P p

Q q

R r

S s

T t

U u

V v

W w

X x

Y y

Z z

■ Can you point to the letter **M**?

■ Can you point to the letter **G**?

E E E E E E E

SHAPES

Can you draw these shapes?

Can you see the **cone**?

Can you draw this shape?

How many sides does a **pentagon** have?

What color is the **heart**?

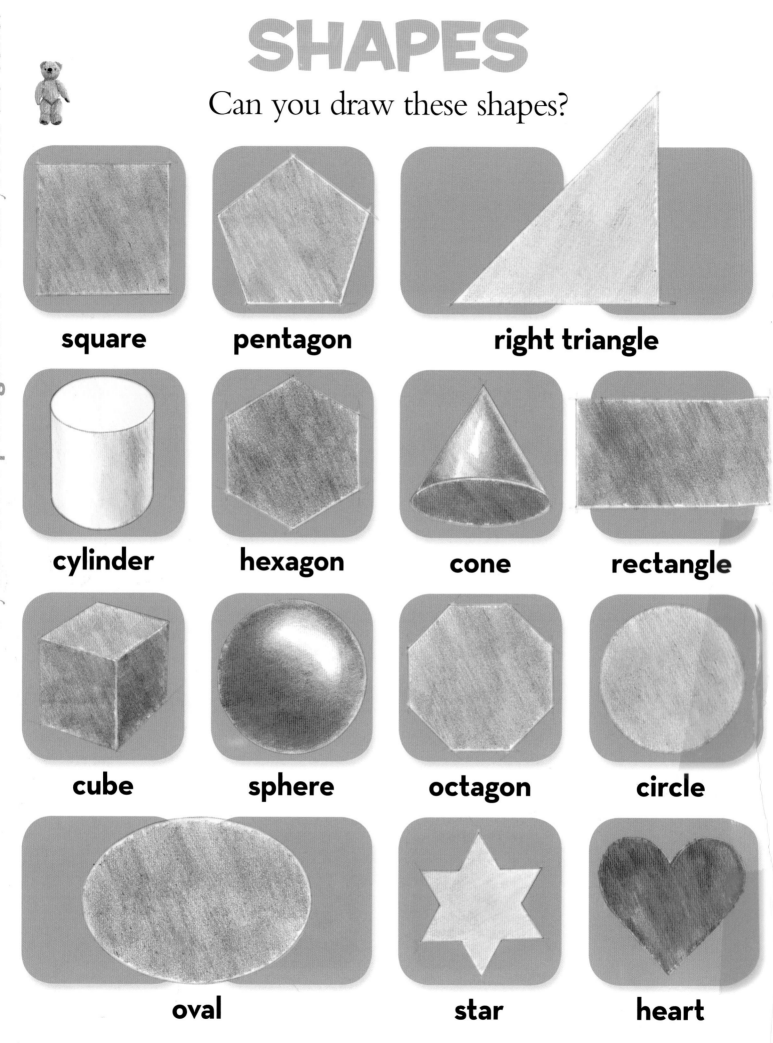

square

pentagon

right triangle

cylinder

hexagon

cone

rectangle

cube

sphere

octagon

circle

oval

star

heart

PATTERNS

What patterns are the bears wearing?

spots   **plaid**

zigzag

checks

wavy   **stars**   **stripes**

COLORS

Which color do you like best?

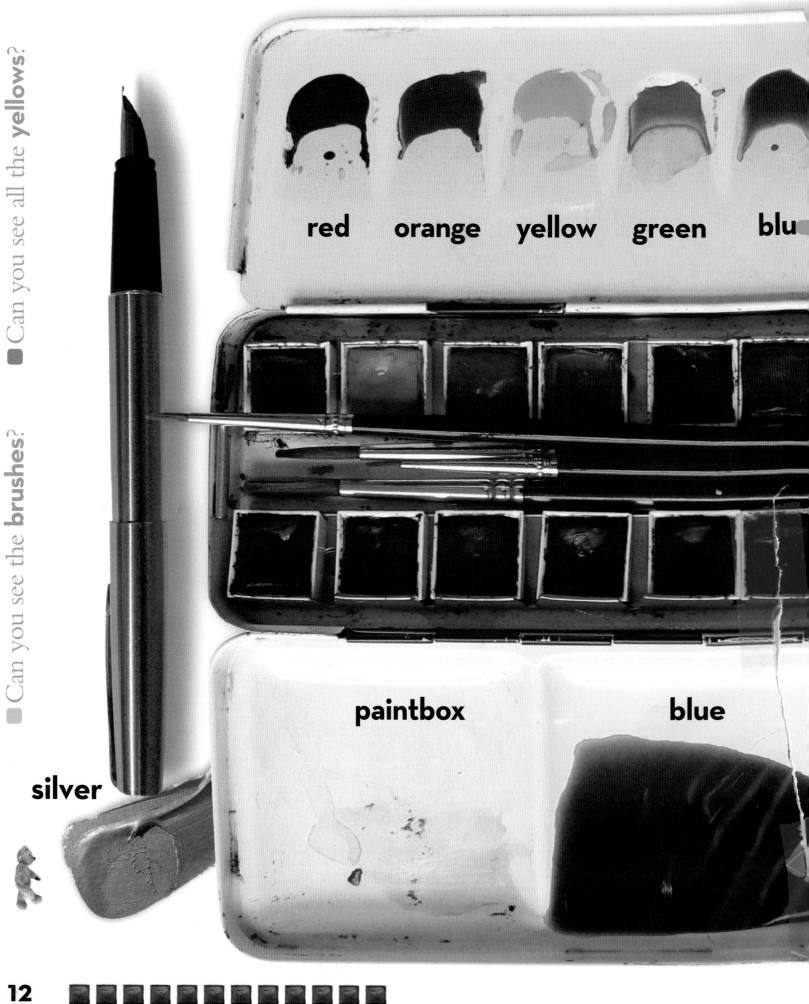

Can you see all the **yellows**?

Can you see the **brushes**?

red   orange   yellow   green   blu

paintbox   blue

silver

pen

urple   pink   brown   gray   black

white

brushes

yellow   red

gold

■ Can you see all the **greens**?   ■ Can you see all the **reds**?

CAR

Are the headlights at the front or back of the car?

rear
window

roof

seat

taillight

What shape are the **wheels**?

back

Where is the **hood**?

bumper

wheel

door handle

● Can you find the **lights**?

● Where is the door **handle**?

steering wheel

side-view mirror

windshield

hood

● What color is the **car**?

front

door

headlight

BODY

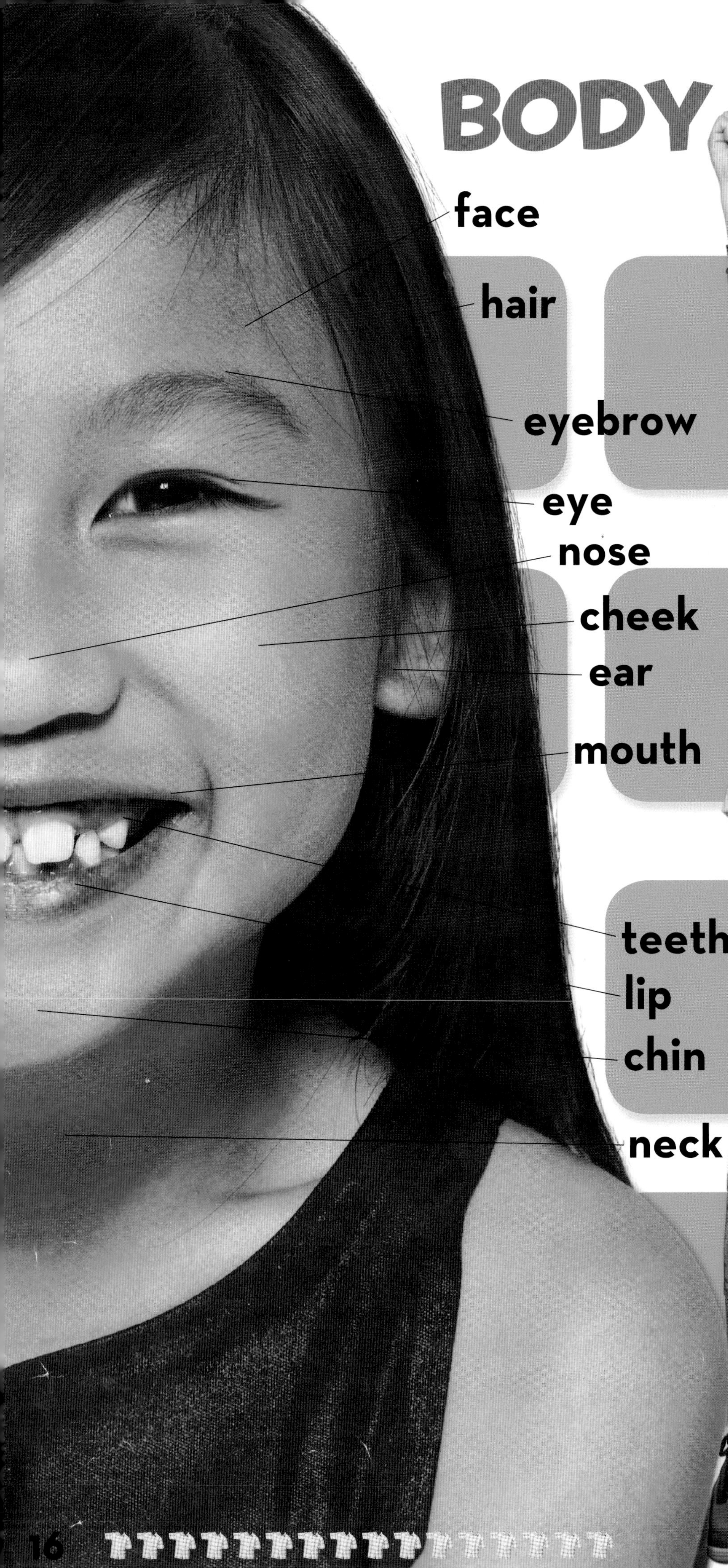

face

hair

eyebrow

eye

nose

cheek

ear

mouth

arm

hand

head

elbow

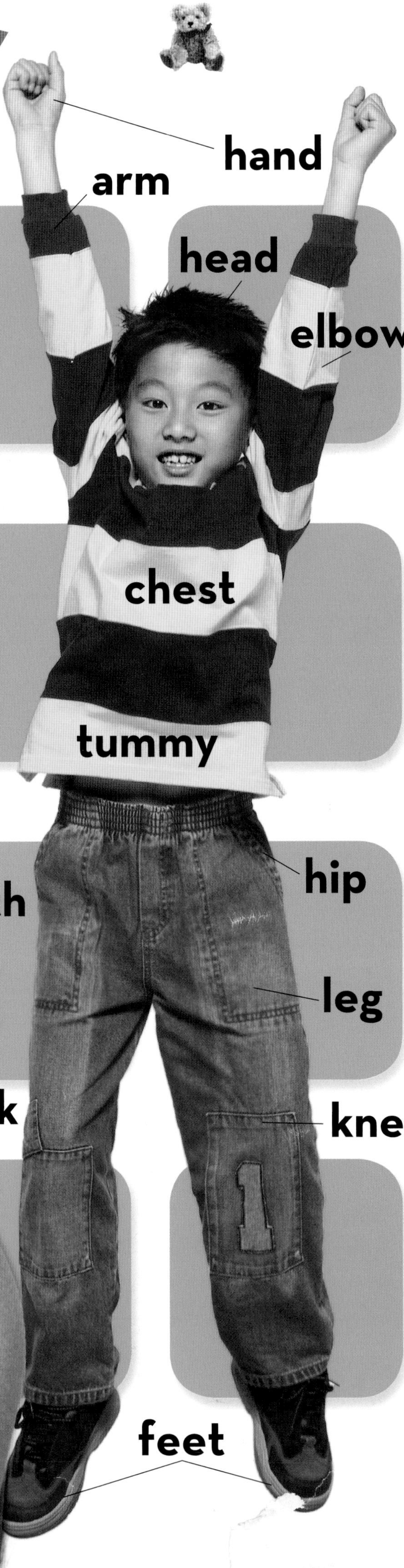

chest

tummy

teeth

lip

chin

hip

leg

neck

knee

feet

CLOTHES

Which boys have shirts with stripes?

shirt

pajamas

shirt

hat

socks

slippers

sweat-shirt

hat

dress

bag

shoes

jeans

school uniform

shorts

sneakers

What color is the **shirt**? What do you wear to **bed**? What color is the boy's **hat**?

THE HOUSE

Can you find these objects in your own home?

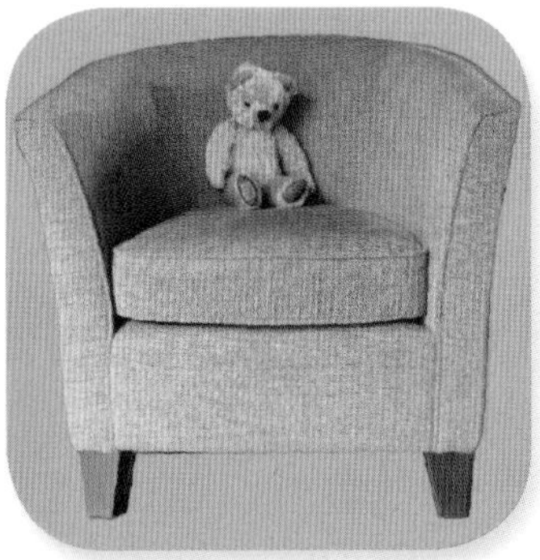

armchair

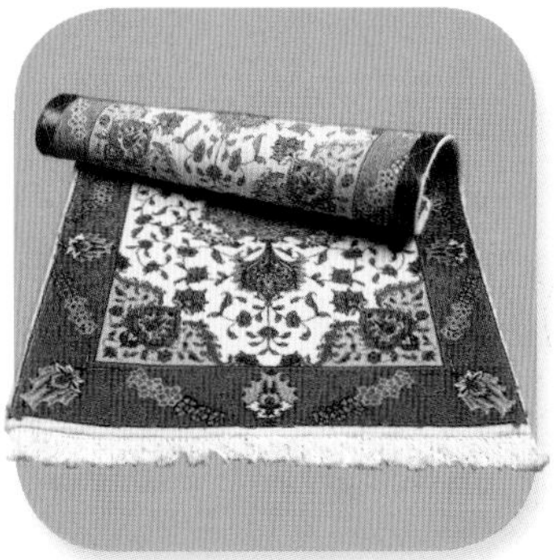

rug

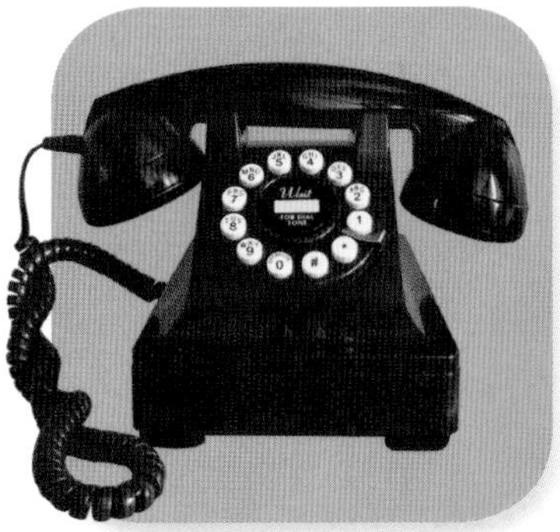

phone

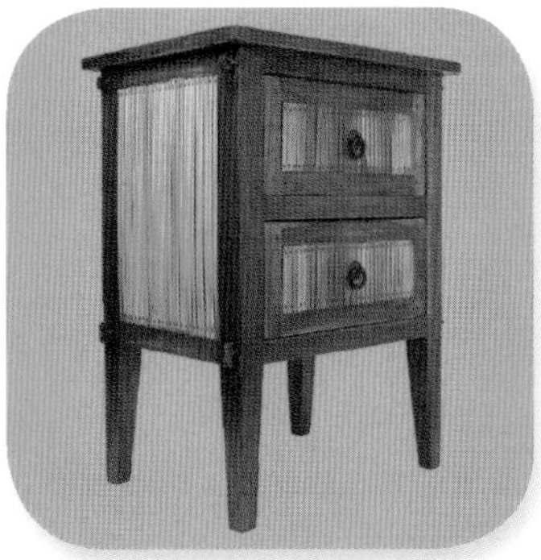

end table

bookcase

book

cushion

computer

clock

sofa

Can you see a **cat**? What time is it on the **clock**? What color is the **telephone**?

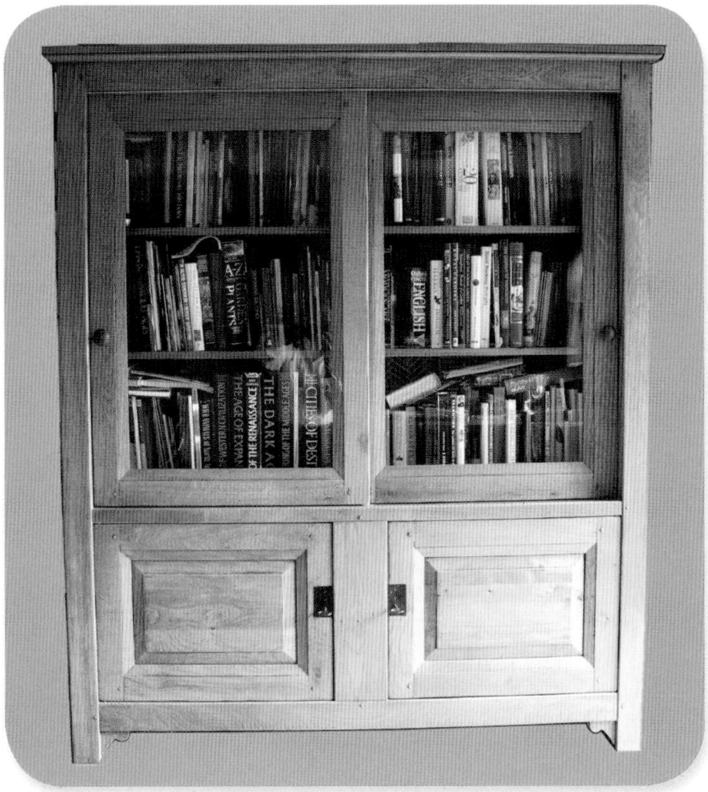

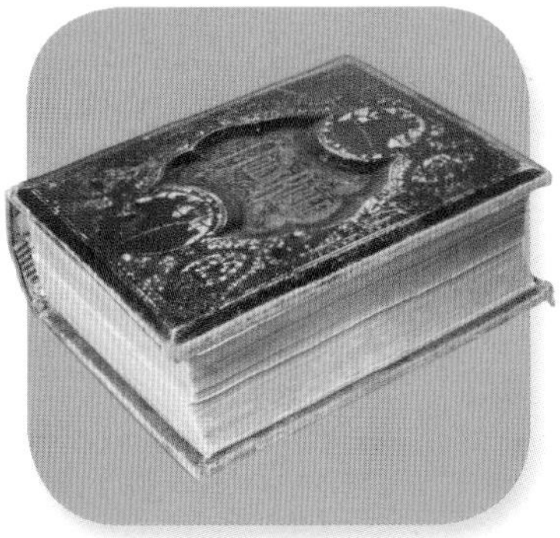

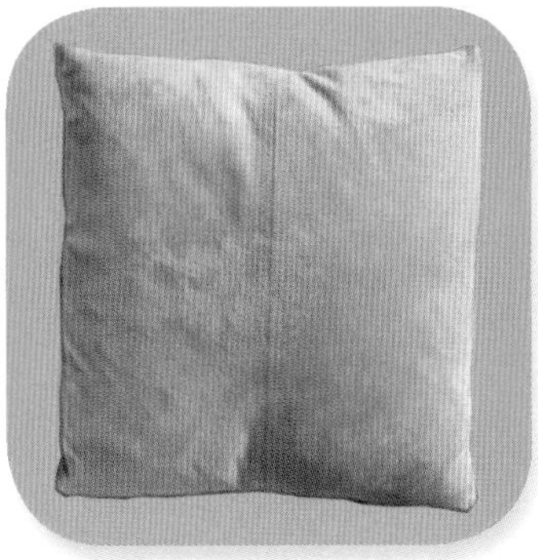

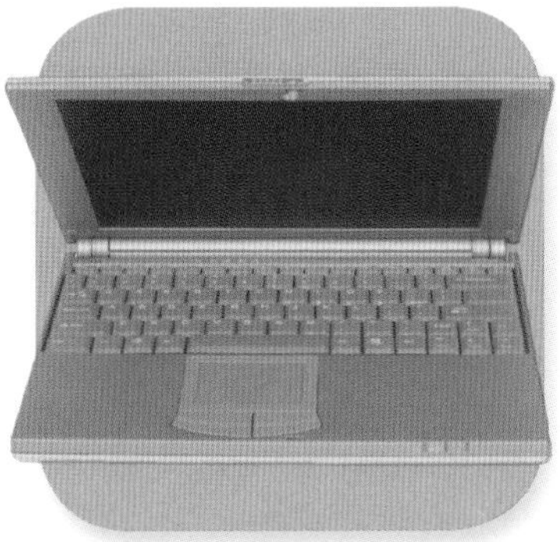

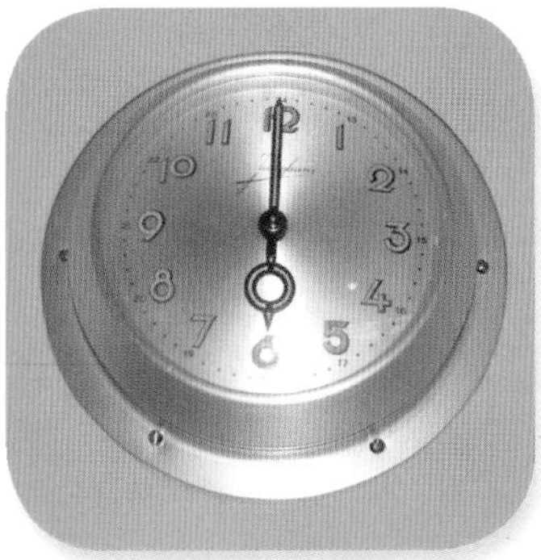

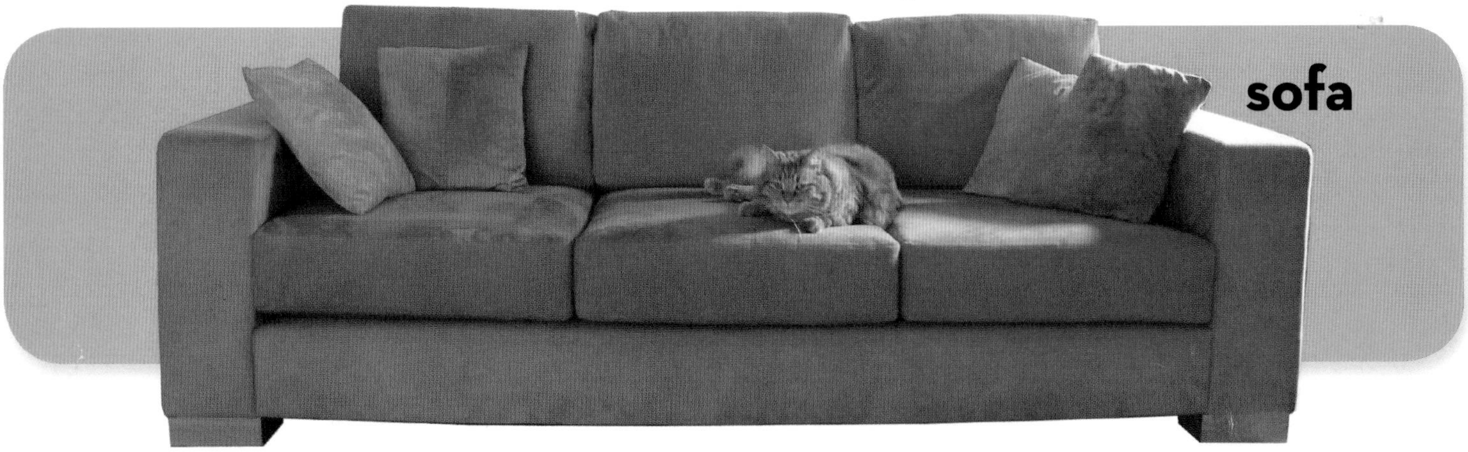

How many **cushions** can you find?

Which do you put **photographs** in?

chimney   **roof**   **window**

wall   **door**   **garage**   **gate**

radio   **flowers**   **keys**   **newspapers**

frames   **television**   **MP3 player**

THE GARDEN

Which object would you use to water plants?

What color is the **rose**?

How many prongs are on the **garden fork**?

rake

garden fork

rose

birdhouse

shears

flowerpot

watering can

bonfire

wheelbarrow

trowel

rubber boots

bush　　　　**sky**　　　　**tree**　　　　**tree house**

■ Can you find a **rake**?

■ What color is the **wheelbarrow**?

flowers　　　　**bench**　　　　**hedge**　　　　**grass**

GOOD MORNING

What time do you wake up?

sun

washcloth

shampoo

toilet paper

brushing your teeth

soap

toothbrush

toothpaste

22

GOOD NIGHT

When do you go to bed?

bed

toilet

teddy

girl

pillows

quilt

pajamas

sleepover

moon

book

sleep

slippers

Where is the **moon**? ▪ Can you find the **soap**? ▪ What pattern is on the **pillows**?

WHAT WE EAT AND DRINK

Which is your favorite **food**?

Can you see the **turkey**?

Where is the **pizza**?

milk

rice

cheese

egg

doughnut

cookies

tacos

cake

sweets

bread

strawberries

steak

scrambled eggs

turkey

salad

hot dog

seafood

pizza

pancake

burger

■ Can you find the **steak**?

■ What color is the **cheese**?

FAMILY AND FRIENDS

How many people are in your family?

Can you see a **mother**?

Can you see a group of **friends**?

grandparents

sister

brother

father and son

mother and daughter

friends

SCHOOL

What subjects do you study at school?

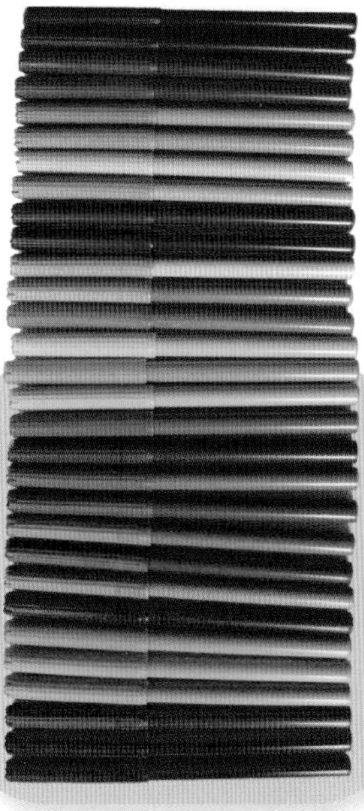

markers

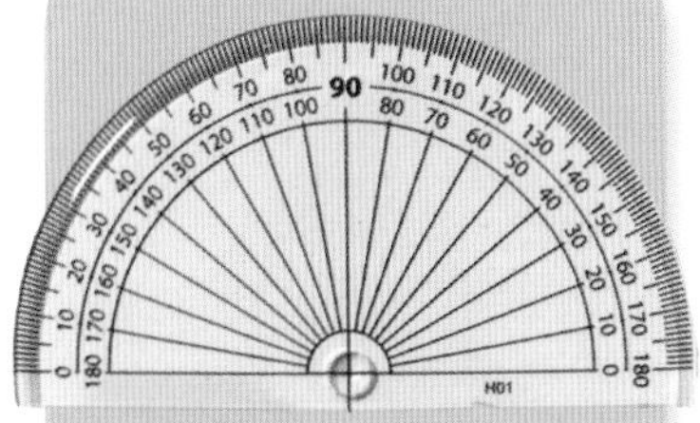

protractor

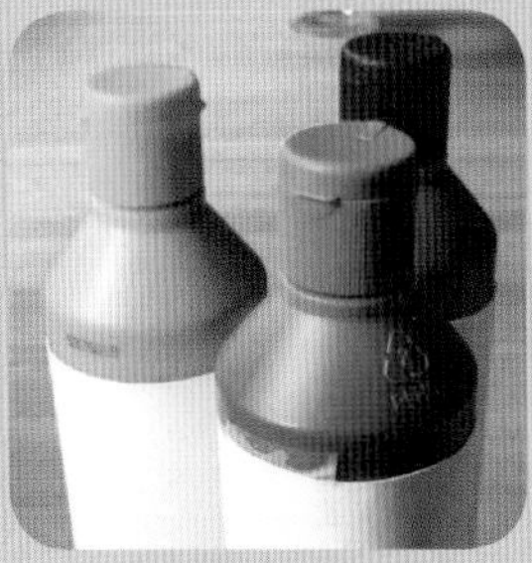

paint

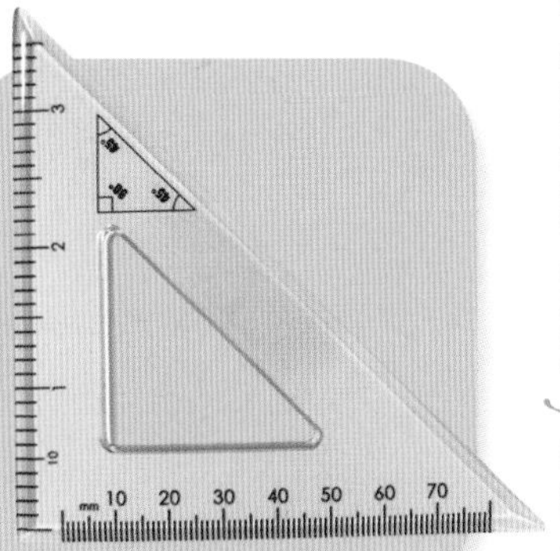

triangle

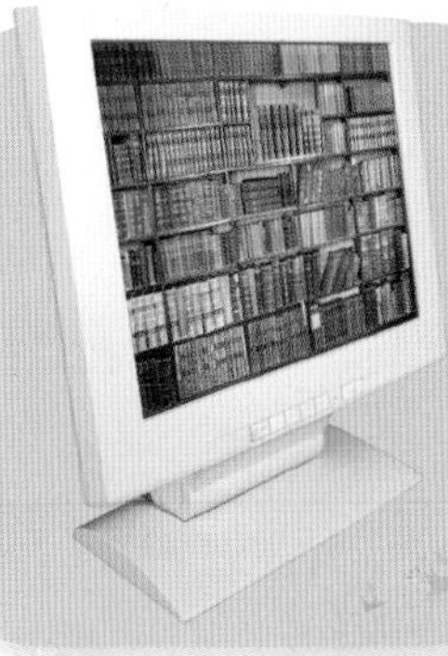

computer

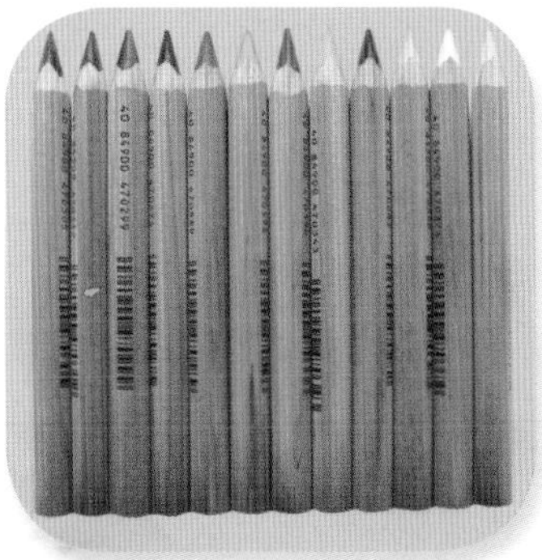

pencils

ruler

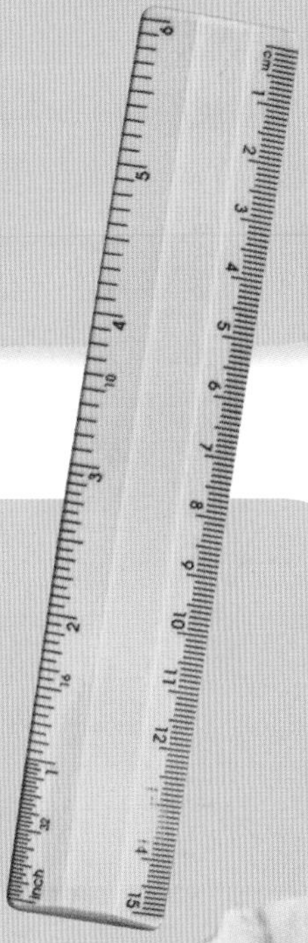

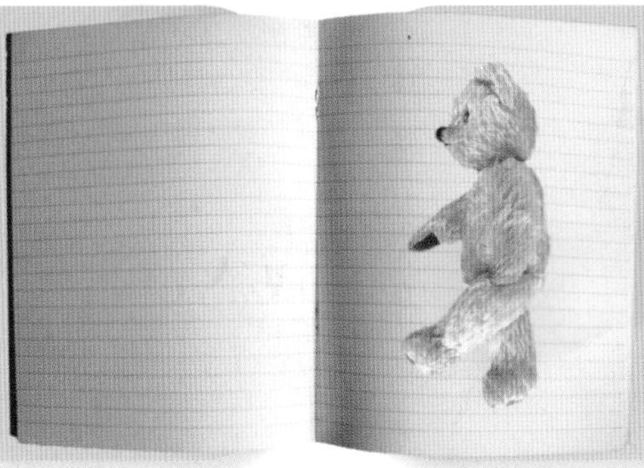

notebook

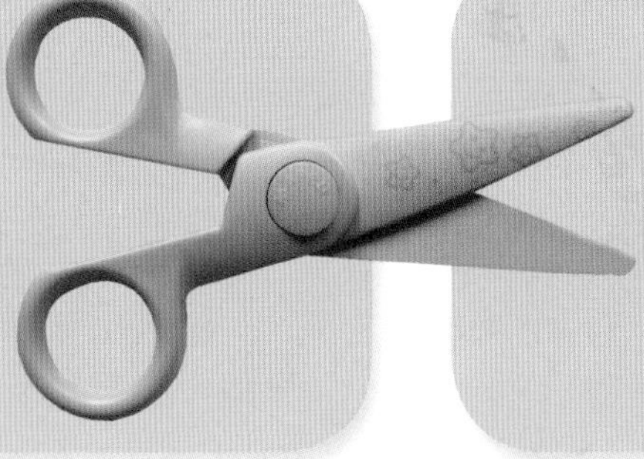

scissors

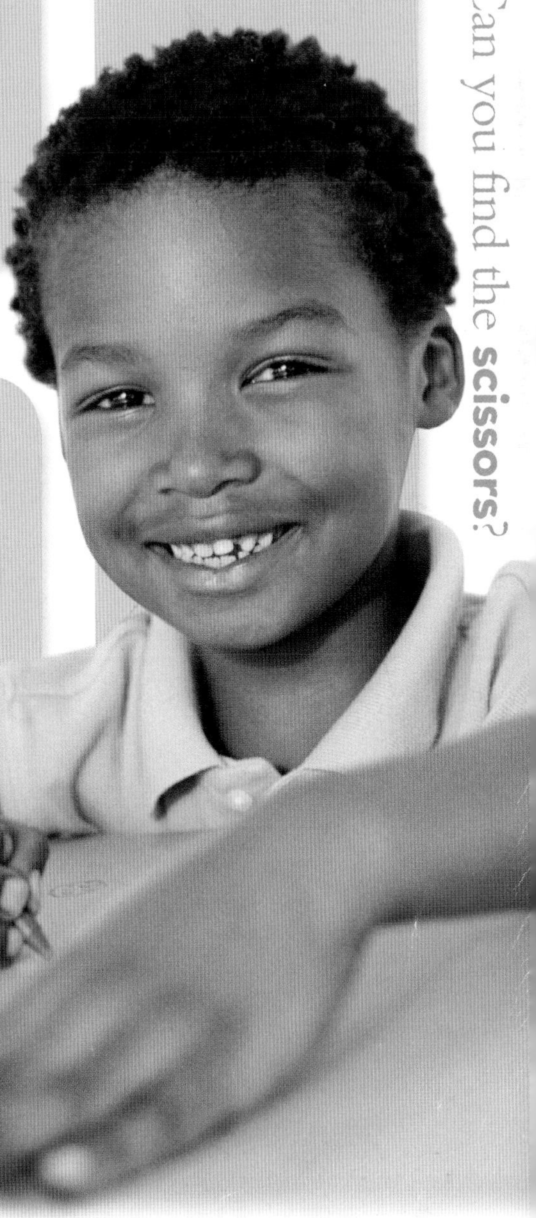

What colors can you **see**?

Can you find the **scissors**?

FUN AND GAMES

What is your favorite game?

Can you find some **cards**?

Can you find things that **bounce**?

robot

soccer ball

drawing

puppet

basketball

cards

bat

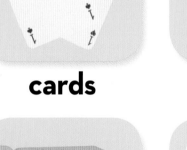

wooden blocks

painting

jump rope

climbing

model plane

jungle gym

What sports do you like?

chess

bubbles

tricycle

balloon

playing soccer

jumping

playing with dolls

robot car

stuffed animals

29

IN THE STREET

What can you find on your street?

street lamp

fire hydrant

speed camera

phone booth

trash can

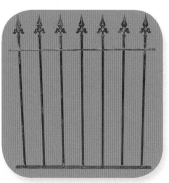
gate

police

statue

construction site

recycling bin

atm

traffic light

firemen

street lamp　　**tower**　　**bridge**　　**window**

● Can you find the telephone **booth**?

■ What colors is the **traffic light**?

sidewalk　　**car**　　**pole**　　**building**

IN THE KITCHEN

What do you use to stir things?

Can you point to the **whisk?**

canned food

pitcher

washing machine

faucet

egg cup

toaster

bowl

dish towel

refrigerator

teapot

saucepan

cereal

■ Where is the **cereal**? ■ Where is the **toaster**?

What can run hot and cold?

knife and fork   **teacup**   **frying pan**

iron

whisk   **oven**

ice cream scoop   **plates**   **kettle**

■ What color is the **teapot**?

■ Can you find a **bowl**?

33

FRUIT

Can you point to the pineapple?

Can you see a **pepper**?

Where is the **orange**?

Can you find a **watermelon**?

bananas

apple

pineapple

lime

pear

grapes

kiwi

lemon

grapefruit

watermelon

peach

orange

tomato

strawberry

cherry

VEGETABLES

Can you find a turnip?

cauliflower

onion

broccoli

mushroom

turnip

potatoes

celery

pepper

string beans

corn

carrots

radishes

lettuce

Where is the **mushroom**? ● Can you see the **potatoes**? ● Can you see a **pear**?

BABY ANIMALS

What is a baby horse called?

kittens

ducklings

foal

calf

piglet

chicks

fawn

puppy

cygnet

lamb

cub

PETS

Do you have any pets?

rabbit

guinea pig

washing the dog

dog

fish

parrot

cat

tortoise

■ Does a **tortoise** move fast or slow? ■ Which pet can **fly**? ■ Can you find a **cat**?

BY THE SEA

What do you use to see underwater?

beach ball

wading

bucket

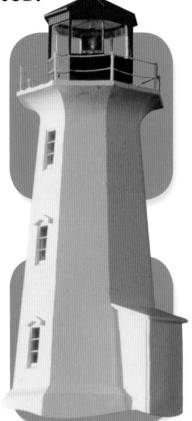

lighthouse

mask

waves

flippers

inflatable tubes

pinwheel

swimming

beach chair

- What can you **dig** with?
- What letter and number can you see on the **fishing boat**?

shell

crab

surfer

fishing boat

beach

sunglasses

- What can you **sit on**?

ON THE FARM

How many animals have two legs?

How many **tractors** can you find?

turkey

duck

donkey

wheat

corn

hen

plowing a field

pig

horseshoe

pony

cow

What color is the rooster's tail?

hay bale

sheep

barn

tractor

rooster

goose

horses

goat

butter churn

■ Can you see the **duck**?

PARTY TIME

What colors are the balloons?

balloons

sandwiches

silver bow

party hat

card

ribbons

gift tag

birthday cake

candle

What color is the **wrapping paper**?

Can you find a red **nose**?

Can you find four hats?

presents

tart

fruit salad

ice cream

clown

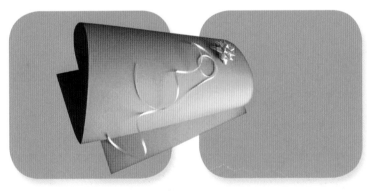

wrapping paper

face paint

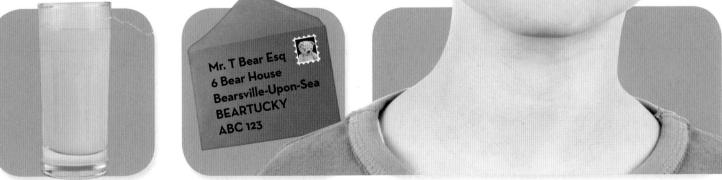

juice

envelope

Mr. T Bear Esq
6 Bear House
Bearsville-Upon-Sea
BEARTUCKY
ABC 123

LET'S MAKE MUSIC

Which instrument has black and white keys?

Where are the **bongos**? ● Can you find a **triangle**? ■ Can you see the **viola**? ●

flute and recorder

tambourine

saxophone

piano

guitar

banjo

microphone

bongos

triangle

violin

bugle

French horn

44

How many instruments have strings?

bagpipes   **drum**   **viola**   **trombone**

How many **drums** can you find?

Can you spot the **guitar**?

musicians

WILD ANIMALS

How many animals have feathers?

Where is the **zebra**? ■ Can you see an **eagle**? ■ How many animals have **stripes**?

panda

crocodile

swan

shark

wolf

cheetah

reindeer

crab

penguin

polar bear

hare

zebra

gorilla

Can you see the crocodile?

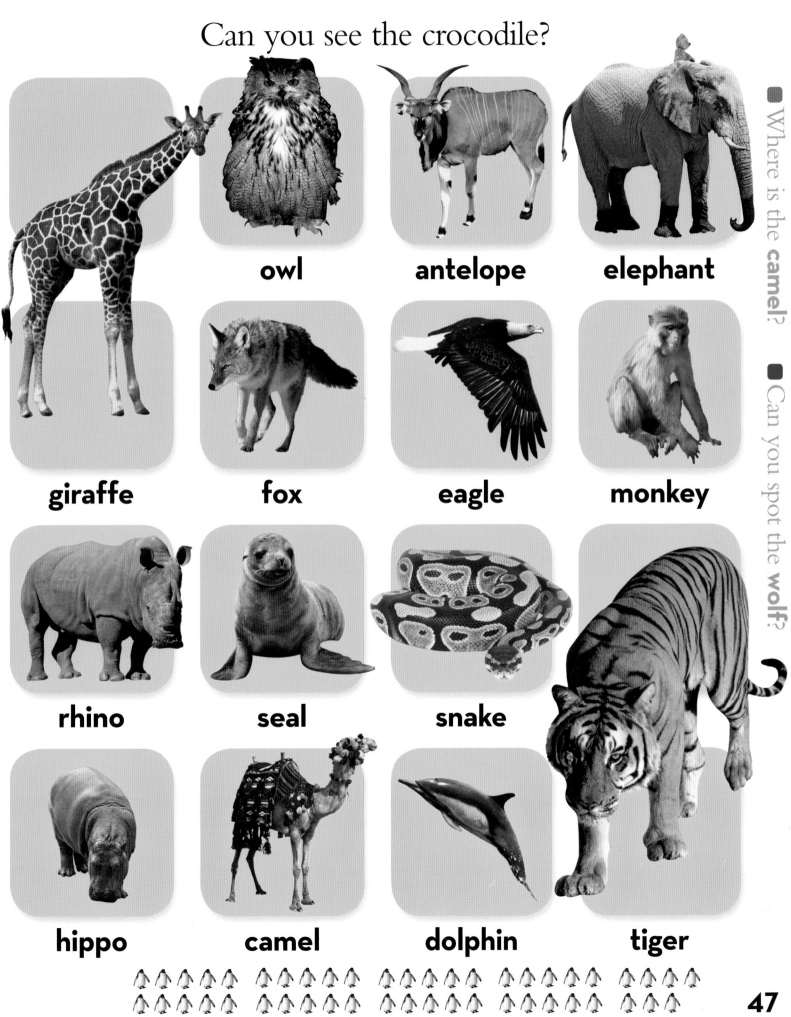

owl

antelope

elephant

giraffe

fox

eagle

monkey

rhino

seal

snake

hippo

camel

dolphin

tiger

■ Where is the **camel**? ■ Can you spot the **wolf**?

ON THE MOVE!

Which of these vehicles can travel on water?

Can you see the **space shuttle**?

train

hot air balloon

boat

Can you see the **plane**?

cruise ship

skateboard

motorcycle

What color is the **car**?

watercraft

hovercraft

plane

snowmobile

raft

Which vehicle travels on snow?

space shuttle

truck

bus

streetcar

bicycle

scooter

car

helicopter

CREEPY CRAWLIES

How many ants can you spot?

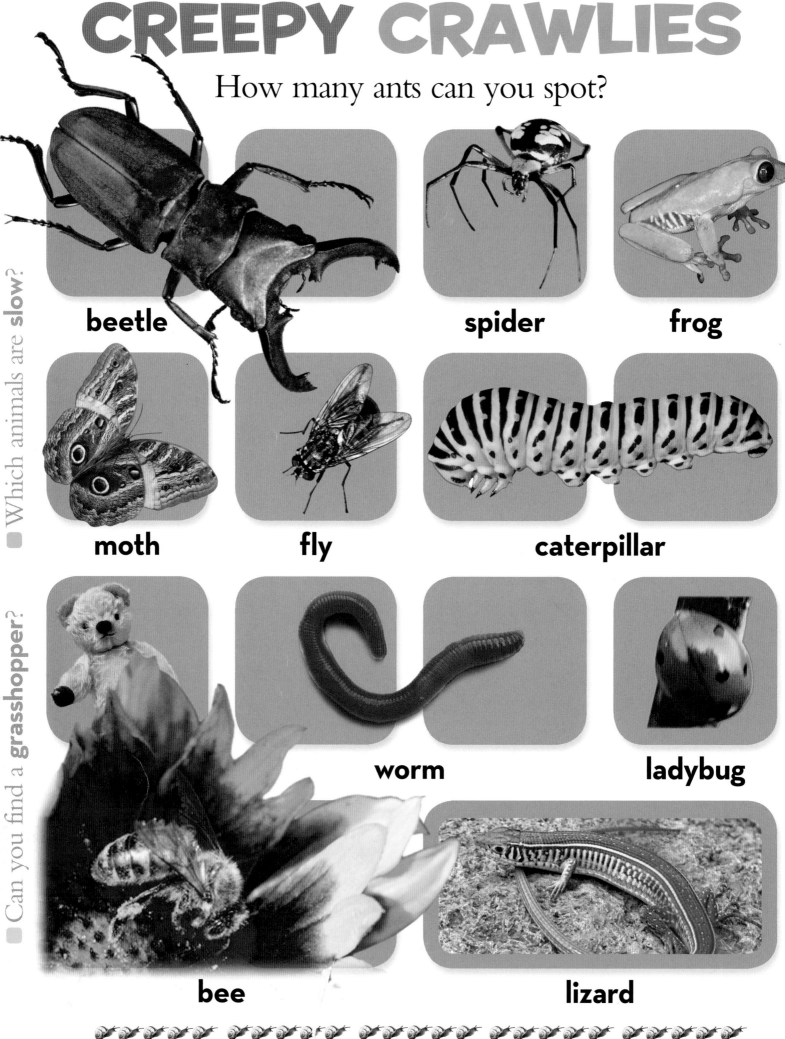

beetle

spider

frog

moth

fly

caterpillar

worm

ladybug

bee

lizard

Where are the two different spiders?

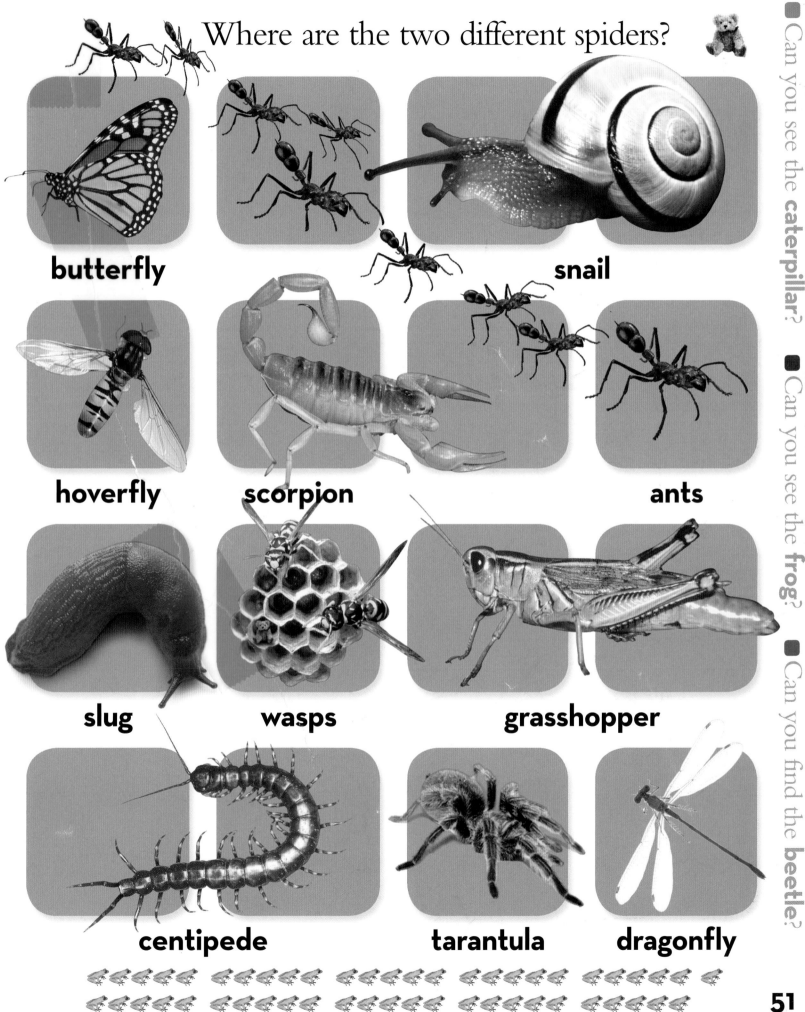

butterfly

snail

hoverfly **scorpion** **ants**

slug **wasps** **grasshopper**

centipede **tarantula** **dragonfly**

I AM BIG!

Where is the **cargo ship**?

Can you see an **iceberg**?

Where is the **tree**?

logging machine

crane

steamroller

rocket

whale

tree

Where is the logging machine?

castle

bison

cargo ship

elephant

airplane

iceberg

● Can you point to the **rocket**?　　● Can you find the **steamroller**?

KramerAllrad 616

bulldozer

SHOPPING

How many men are getting haircuts?

bakery

candy store

grocery store

craft store

delicatessen

barbershop

fabric store

fish market

butcher shop

flower shop

toy store

music store

dress shop

How many carrots do you see?

farmers market

Can you point to the **green beans**?

Can you spot the **radishes**?

IN THE WORKSHOP

What color is the oil can?

Can you find the **hammer**?

Where is the **vise**?

Where is the **paintbrush**?

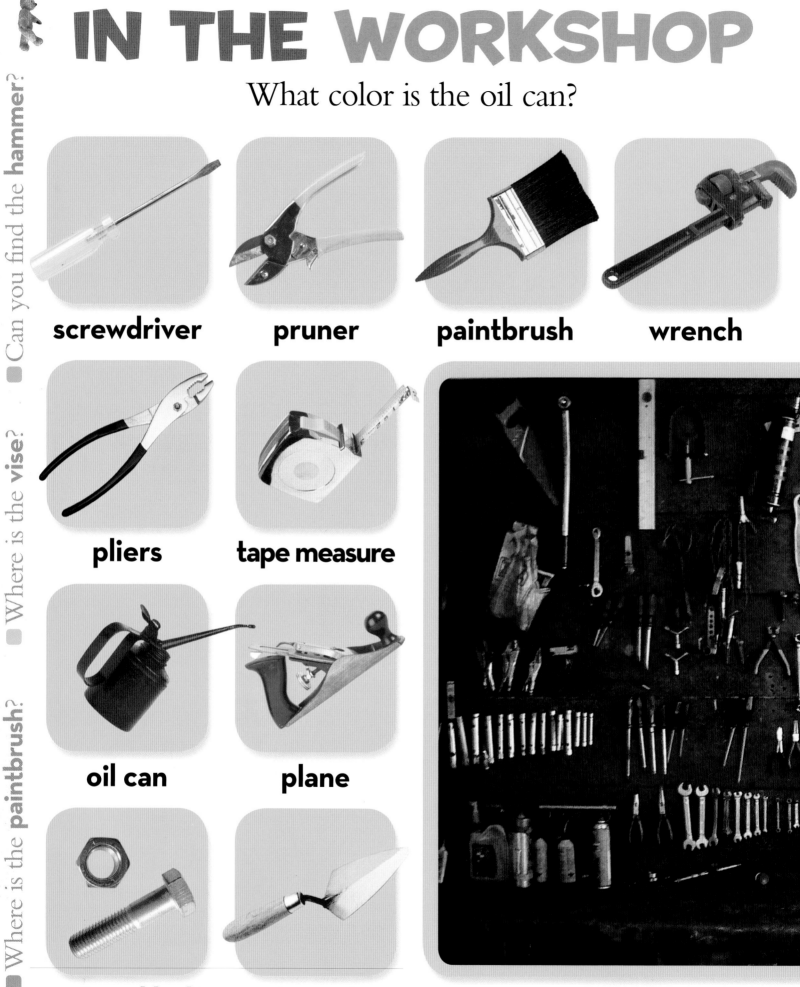

screwdriver

pruner

paintbrush

wrench

pliers

tape measure

oil can

plane

nut and bolt

trowel

workshop

Are there eight wrenches in the set?

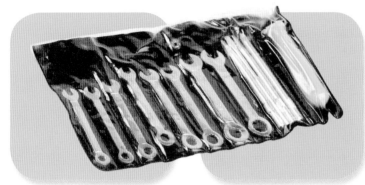

set of wrenches

toolbox

axe

saw

hammer

vise

bench

electric drill

OUT AND ABOUT

Where would you go to catch a plane?

Where would you find lots of **buildings**?

Can you find a **bridge**?

mountain

city

waterfall

river

bridge

Where would you find lots of boats?

highway

buildings

canal

airport

train station

lake

harbor

WEATHER

Where is the **flood**? ◼ Can you see the **fog**? ◼ Where is the **tornado**? ◼

umbrella

hurricane

tornado

lightning

raincoat

snow

flood

rainbow

fog

60

SEASONS

Which season follows winter?

spring

summer

fall

winter

TIME

 How many hours are there in a day?

What time is **lunch?** ● When is **playtime?** ● What time is **dinner?**

nighttime

wake-up time

morning time

breakfast time

bedtime

clock

school time

toothbrush time

lunchtime

dinnertime

playtime

going home time

class time

INDEX

How many words start with the letter E?

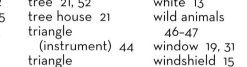

INDEX

Can you see "shark?"
Can you find "yellow?"
How many words start with "Q?"

Created, designed, and edited for Salariya by:
Elizabeth Branch
Stephen Haynes
David Stewart
Rob Walker
Mark Williams

For the National Geographic Society
Priyanka Lamichhane, *Project Editor*
Jonathan Halling, *Design Director*
Kathryn Robbins, *Design Production Assistant*
Lori Epstein, *Senior Illustrations Editor*

First published in North America in 2011 by National Geographic Society
1145 17th Street N.W.
Washington, D.C. 20036-4688

Library of Congress Cataloging-in-Publication Data
Word book: learning the words in your world.
p. cm.
Includes index.
ISBN 978-1-4263-0789-8 (alk. paper)
ISBN 978-1-4263-0790-4 (library binding : alk. paper)
1. Vocabulary. I. National Geographic Society (U.S.)
PE1449.W623 2011
428.1--dc22
2010049462

Photo credits: Banana Stock Ltd, Brand X Pictures, Corbis, Digital Stock Corporation, Digital Vision, Ingram Publishing, iStockphoto, John Foxx Images, Jonathan Salariya, Shutterstock, Photodisc, Power Photos

Printed in China
11/SAL/1

Printed on paper from sustainable sources.

PAPER FROM
SUSTAINABLE FORESTS

Answer to question on page 5: 72 bears